COMING APART

• • • • • • • • • • • • • •

COMING TOGETHER

COMING
APART

● ● ● ● ● ● ● ● ● ● ●

COMING
TOGETHER

ONE MAN'S JOURNEY
OUT OF DEPRESSION

ANDREW PAIGE

One Liguori Drive
Liguori, MO 63057-9999
(314) 464-2500

LIGUORI
PUBLICATIONS

ISBN 0-89243-540-2
Library of Congress Catalog Card Number: 93-79274

Copyright © 1994, Liguori Publications
Printed in the United States of America

Cover design by Chris Sharp

About the author:
Andrew Paige knows the terrors of depression firsthand. His own experience with depression lasted for nearly a year, during which he was almost completely overcome with despair. In this book, Paige shares his experience of hope and healing. As a trained psychotherapist and a noted clergyman, Paige writes under a pseudonym to protect his privacy and the privacy of those who walked with him through the darkness back into the light.

This book is dedicated to Kirk and Lois,
who daily lead people
from darkness into the light.

From all of us:
thank you!

Contents

Introduction

This book is about a journey—a long journey from darkness to light, from pain to peace, from disintegration to a new sense of wholeness. It has not been an easy book to write. Reliving past experiences of pain is, in and of itself, painful. Memories can hurt, and in the process of writing this, many did.

And yet, I want to tell my story—I had to tell my story—not only for myself but for those who have made, are making, and will make the journey into the dark valley of depression. If this book helps make the journey easier, the stay shorter, and the way out more accessible for even one pilgrim, it will have achieved its purpose.

I also write for those who will suffer mild experiences of depression and for those who minimize depression as an illness. May this book help you better understand those of us who have come apart from the onslaught of depression. Most of us will come back together, restored to wholeness; sadly, some will not. Like most serious illnesses, depression leaves both survivors and casualties. Untreated—and occasionally when treated—depression can be as much a killer as cancer.

Understanding, compassion, acceptance, and love constitute the strongest medicine. I ask all of you who read this book to generously share these gifts with those experiencing depression; they desperately need your support.

Telling my story is part of my own healing process. In remembering and expressing the memories, it becomes clear that God was present—never absent—throughout the entire journey. Rather, God's quiet presence was and remains the source of grace that resurrects, renews, and restores. In the midst of the darkness and pain, "Where are you, God?" rips the lining of the soul. Remembering the pain and telling the story answers the question—and the answer is "I am here."

Telling my story has also put me in touch with a genuine understanding and appreciation for the meaning of salvation. Although I am fully responsible for myself and my behavior, I cannot save myself. Salvation, today and eternally, remains a gift. The same is true with the struggle against depression. We do what we can; with vigor and perseverance, we pour our total essence into coping with its stranglehold. And part of that struggle means reaching out for, asking for, and accepting the help we desperately need.

I invite you to join your story with mine. Together, we become a tool for healing. Sharing our journeys and telling our stories puts us in touch with the power of the illness and gives us hope for recovery—for ourselves and for others.

Andrew Paige

I write under a pseudonym to protect those who have journeyed with me through the dark grip of depression. I am a priest with a high visibility; anonymity allows me a greater freedom of expression and provides a measure of sensitivity for the privacy of others.

COMING APART

PART I

I

"Priests Don't Get Depressed" and Other Myths

I remember both conversations well. They occurred only a few weeks apart, several years before my episode of major depression.

The first conversation took place after I asked a small Bible-study group to pray for a priest-friend of mine who had been hospitalized for depression. The group appeared genuinely surprised.

One of the more vocal participants, a sweet little Irish lady, spoke up. "Father," she said, "I never realized priests got depressed. Goodness, you would think with all the faith you priests have, there wouldn't be any room for depression."

The other conversation took place with a prominent Catholic psychiatrist I met at an ethics workshop. In our conversations, I shared with him the condition of my sick priest-friend. He nodded understandingly. "Over the years," he said, "I've treated a good many priests for depression. In fact, depression seems quite common in your profession."

When I asked him why, he looked at me reflectively. "There is probably no single reason," he replied, "because depression occurs when a number of factors converge. For example, priests are alone a lot and may not feel supported or affirmed. Sometimes they drink too much. Or it could be a combination of a lot of things: too many transfers, too much work, too little genuine intimacy with too much loneliness, too many demands on too little resources.

"I guess I would say," he added, "that another factor is the sensitivity of you men. Priesthood is a caring profession, but sometimes you care too much and get overwhelmed. You start internalizing the stress, and the problems and hurts you see every day get under your skin and won't go away. You begin to feel helpless about things you can't really change. Over time, that sense of helplessness turns into anger, and since there's no place for the anger to go, it surfaces as depression."

He paused for a moment, then continued.

"Mainly, depression is a response to the loss of hope. And just like the rest of us, priests can and do lose hope. That's when depression can take over, and in fact, it usually does."

Three years later, when the darkness of depression gripped my own inner spaces, I would remember the accuracy of his observations.

Myths Surrounding Depression

In spite of all the progress that has been made in educating people about mental health and mental illness, depression remains poorly understood and continues to be surrounded by myths.

A real man or a strong woman doesn't get depressed, at least not for long. This myth is especially damaging to the person struggling with depression. The fact is, depression is not the manifestation of a character defect or a human weakness. A person struggling with depression is not a wimp or an emotional weakling.

Granted, everyone has bad days, but depression is not a "bad-day" experience. "Pull yourself together, cheer up, snap out of it. Take charge of your life. You can do it by yourself if you just try hard enough. Exercise some will power. Depression disappears once you order it to go away and you get on with living. You don't have to be depressed unless you choose to be. And if you choose to be, then don't gripe about it." These quips stem from the "bad-day" mind-set that trivializes the effects of the illness and adds to the pain.

The husband of a couple coming to me for marriage counseling complained about his wife's depression, accusing his wife of "using" depression to avoid the responsibilities of marriage. The husband ignored the fact that his wife had a long history of depression and had, in fact, been treated for depression before they were married. It was obvious that the wife was in the grips of major depression, but her husband was blinded by the "bad-day" myth.

When I recommended that the wife seek therapy and a medical evaluation for possible hospitalization, the husband refused to cooperate. "We'll work it out," he insisted. "I don't want everyone in town saying my wife is a mental case."

Shortly after we talked, the husband was transferred to another state. The move was devastating to his wife's health. Living in an unfamiliar community and far from what little support she enjoyed, his wife's depression worsened. One quiet, sunny morning, her husband at work and her children at school, the illness of depression proved terminal: she took her own life. This woman became another unnecessary casualty of the "bad-day" myth that sabotages so many hopes for recovery.

A strong faith wards off depression. This myth, enshrined in religious overtones, is especially debilitating. It's one thing to struggle with depression as a character weakness, like the first

15

myth suggests, but admitting to a lack of faith reaches deep into a person's faith core. Guilt, fear, and hopelessness result.

Because this myth is so convincing, it is difficult for congregations to accept the fact that their religious leaders can suffer depression. Since I am a trained psychotherapist as well as a clergy, non-Catholic clergy often seek me out for therapy. Invariably, they are concerned about confidentiality. They tell me that if their congregation finds out they suffer from depression, they could lose their jobs, or at least be rendered unreliable as leaders of the faithful.

A religious leader can suffer from high blood pressure, diabetes, even alcoholism, but not depression. Depression among the clergy has not yet come out of the closet; it is not a fashionable ailment. Depression remains something to be ashamed of because the myth says "People of faith do not become depressed. They have God! If they do become depressed, then their walk with God is obviously questionable."

The Fact: Depression Is an Illness

Depression is an illness that respects neither believers nor non-believers. It is an "equal-opportunity" affliction; saint or sinner, you can become depressed to the point of preferring death to another day of darkness.

Elijah, a great holy man of God and one of the foremost saints of the Old Testament, knew depression. In the Book of Kings, we are given a powerful description of his depressed state: fatigue, disturbed sleep, poor appetite patterns, and a desire for death.

Elijah went a day's journey into the desert, where he came to a broom tree and sat beneath it. He prayed for death:

"Enough, O Lord! Take my life, for I am no better than my fathers." He lay down and slept under the broom tree, but then an angel touched him and ordered him to get up and eat. He looked and there at his head was a hearth cake and a jug of water. After he ate and drank, he lay down again, but the angel of the Lord came back a second time, touched him, and ordered, "Get up and eat, else the journey will be too long for you!" Elijah got up, ate and drank; then strengthened by that food, he walked forty days and forty nights to the mountain of God, Horeb.

1 Kings 19:3-8

In Catholic tradition, the lives of the saints are replete with examples of holy men and women who struggled heroically against depression: Elizabeth Ann Seton, Catherine of Siena, Ignatius of Loyola, and Therese of Lisieux, to name just a few.

Four hundred years before the birth of modern psychiatry, Ignatius offered an uncannily accurate description of one source of desolation which might be described as depression. Particularly interesting is this quote from *The Spiritual Exercises of St. Ignatius.* He believed desolation to be a part of everyone's life sooner or later.

I call desolation...darkness of soul, turmoil of spirit, inclination to what is low and earthy, restlessness rising from many disturbances and temptations which lead to want of faith, want of hope, want of love. The soul is wholly slothful, tepid, sad, and separated, as it were, from its Creator and Lord.

As she lay dying from tuberculosis, suffering excruciating mental and physical pain, Saint Therese of Lisieux came to un-

17

derstand how those who experience chronic suffering might want to commit suicide and end it all.

> When one suffers like this, it would take only an instant to lose one's reason, and the deed would be done *(The Story of a Soul)*.

I remember a wise and holy priest saying to a group of us priests, "When you are sick, it is usually hard to pray, and it may be even harder to believe God exists. If he does exist, why is he letting you suffer this way? Never demand too much of those who are ill because there is little they have to give. And be extra sensitive to their plight. Remember: some day you may share their experience."

Faith can be assaulted and battered when serious illness strikes, and that is exactly what clinical depression is: a serious illness. In fact, one of depression's unique features is the ability to make everything, including one's relationship with God, seem flat, empty, and meaningless.

Depression makes it difficult to focus on God—or anything. Depression saps energy, makes one feel worthless, and immobilizes every area of life. From the midst of depression, nothing seems to function properly, including faith—and that adds further pain. Persons struggling with depression don't need to hear, "This must be God's will for you" or "Hang in there; suffering builds character." Persons in the dark grip of depression don't need simplistic solutions to their pain. They need patience, compassion, and professional help—and the sooner the better.

Treatment

Depression should be treated as exactly what it is: a significant health disorder, a debilitating condition, an illness.

Fortunately, persons suffering from depression respond remarkably well to a variety of treatment modalities. Eighty percent of those treated for depression are able to resume normal, satisfying lives.

Shortly after I was ordained, I visited one of my former associate pastors, Father Tom, who was newly discharged from a psychiatric facility where he had been treated for severe depression. He looked good and sounded strong. During the course of our conversation, he said to me with a laugh, "I may have been crazy, Andy, but I was never dumb. I knew it was time to get help for my depression, and thank God, I did. I'm a new man today."

Tom was appointed pastor of a large parish and went on to function as a competent priest for many years. I admire Tom for the courage he showed in facing mental illness during a time when there was still considerable stigma attached to it.

To me, Tom was one of those providentially provided role models who leaves us examples of courage—grace under pressure. Years later, I would ponder his strength when, at the very height of my career as a priest-psychotherapist, the "black dog of depression" (as Winston Churchill referred to it) attacked with a vengeance. As its dark claws tore me apart, causing unimaginable inner pain to my mind and spirit, the memory of Tom's courage forestalled my desire for death.

I'm not, by nature, a myth destroyer, but this book is meant to destroy the two myths that contribute to the needless suffering of countless victims of depression. Depression is not a "bad day"; it is a serious mental illness. Depression is not affiliated with one's depth of faith; anyone can fall victim to its icy grip. I did—and this is my story.

II

Tunnel at the End of the Light

It was Tuesday, November 6, 1990. I awoke from a troubled sleep to find myself enveloped in a thick mental fog that no light penetrated and no power of my own diffused. The darkest journey of my life was under way, for on that morning I began to grope my way through a tunnel of inner darkness, where moving forward only meant more darkness. Before my journey's end, I despaired of ever seeing light again.

The darkness was an episode of major depression, and it was to pull me apart and nearly kill me. For the next ten months, I would stagger through life in a state of emotional disequilibrium, uncertain of myself, feeling powerless and hopeless, struggling desperately to find enough meaning to validate my existence. My inner battle, witnessed by only a select few, would hold an uncertain outcome to the very end.

Like a physician reading his own electrocardiogram during a heart attack, I knew what was happening to me that gray November morning. I knew that depression had sunk its teeth into me and was shaking me like a rag doll. I also knew that it would not let go easily.

I thought I was experiencing a surprise attack by an old enemy. What I did not know then was that it had launched a full-scale war upon me, and not to win was to die.

Depression and Your Family History

Sometimes an illness provides us with a lens through which we can look back on our lives. It may actually help us interpret the past with greater clarity and explain events that, at the time, made little sense.

In one form or another, I had been skirmishing with depression for years. My family has a long history of depression on both my father's and my mother's sides, a history that can be traced back four generations. Both my father and my mother lost a brother to depression-related suicide.

Other members of my family, especially my numerous cousins, have battled depression for years; many are still on antidepressants and in therapy. Most have realized encouraging results, but some have not. A few years ago, I buried a twenty-four-year-old cousin who battled depression that began in his adolescence. The illness steadily wore him down until finally, his spirit crushed, he took his own life.

My maternal grandmother's life was ruined by depression. Following the birth of my mother, my grandmother experienced devastating postpartum depression with psychotic features, including delusions and hallucinations. Because other relatives feared she might be a threat to her small children, she was taken to a state hospital where she spent the rest of her life, dying at age sixty-two.

Years later, when I was a chaplain at that hospital, I had the opportunity to read her file. I remember being awed by the virulence of the depression that had so mercilessly robbed her of her mind and plunged her into total madness.

My mother, now deceased, was also a victim of depression. My only sibling, a sister, died at age twelve, when I was five years old.

That death catapulted my mother into profound grieving. In unguarded moments, my mother would talk about the seven-year grieving period she underwent after my sister's death. It was a time marked by deep depression. The only things that kept her going, she admits, were her need to raise me and her faith in God.

The loss of my sister did not diminish Mother's walk with God. Instead, Mother's faith seemed to deepen. She believed strongly in eternal life and in reunion with our loved ones. These promises of God sustained her through this, the worst period of her life.

Undoubtedly because of our family history, Mother was deeply empathic with others as they struggled with the darkness of depression. She was drawn to those who were hurting emotionally, doing whatever she could to support them. It may have been something as simple as baking a tray of cookies for the person in pain, but her attempts were genuine and often sustaining.

On one occasion, Mother brought home an elderly lady who had spent years hospitalized for depression. Mother provided the woman with care until she was reunited with her family.

I recall the long weeks Mother spent helping a large family after the mother suffered a nervous breakdown and was sent to the state hospital for electroconvulsive therapy: "shock treatment," as it was called then.

Mother became incensed when people made fun of the mentally ill; she knew full well that mental illness was no laughing matter, that it wreaked havoc in human lives. In her own quiet way, Mother was an advocate for the mentally ill her entire adult life.

Professionally, Mother was a teacher, but she was drawn to helping others with their emotional struggles. If she had chosen another field, I think it would have been psychology. Armed with that knowledge, she could have developed a more extensive set of skills in assisting the emotionally disturbed.

Raised in this kind of environment, it is understandable that I developed a deep compassion for those struggling with emotional disturbances. Along with the required theology, I took as much psychology as I could while I studied for the priesthood. I knew it would be an invaluable asset in working with people.

My first personal encounter with major depression took place two years after I was ordained. I began to realize considerable personal stress, both in the rectory that I shared with two other priests and in the parish ministry itself. I suffered from high anxiety, poor sleep habits, overwhelming sadness, and intense feelings of helplessness and hopelessness. Gradually, my functioning became impaired; it was difficult to carry out the routine duties of parish work.

Finally, as my desperation mounted, I turned to my personal physician for help. He recognized the depression but could prescribe only an older group of antidepressant medications that have most unfavorable side effects. Within three days, I knew I wouldn't be able to tolerate the medication. The side effect I most feared manifested itself: excessive dry mouth. My mouth felt as though it were stuffed with cotton, and I was virtually unable to swallow or talk. For someone who spoke publicly every day, it was the worst possible reaction to the medicine. The medication had to go.

It did, and I was again left to the ravages of the disease without defense.

Next, I decided to see a psychiatrist. Unfortunately, this, too, turned out to be a dead end. The psychiatrist failed to recognize the depths of my depression and prescribed tranquilizers for the anxiety. The medication helped me sleep but did not address the deeper problems. As a result, I continued to fall further into the tunnel at the end of the light.

Then God intervened.

Although my bishop had no knowledge of my condition, he called during the height of my depression. He invited me to take time away from parish settings and return to school for some additional training. I jumped at the chance. Away from the major stresses I had been experiencing in my living situation and in parish ministry, the depression lifted.

Several years later, I told my bishop what had happened and how his intervention must have been inspired by God. He laughed heartily and said, "I guess the Holy Spirit really does work through me sometimes."

An Environment for Depression

Over the years, I found myself working with so many depressed persons that I began to feel overwhelmed and inadequate. Those who came to me for guidance and counseling were grateful for the time and help I gave them, but too often I did not see any significant changes in their lives. I wondered if perhaps I could do more for them with additional training.

On the eleventh anniversary of my ordination, I went to my bishop and asked permission to return to graduate school to pursue a master's degree in social work. I wanted to integrate my basic theological understanding with psychology to form what I described as a "psychospiritual" approach to pastoral ministry, with a strong emphasis on soul and mind healing: inner healing.

My bishop was skeptical and not enthusiastic about releasing me for two years to study at a secular university. He finally agreed, however, provided I covered my own expenses.

A year and a half later, and twenty thousand dollars poorer, I was back in my diocese with a master's degree in social work and many new insights about the treatment of depression. When I put these newly acquired skills to work in pastoral settings, I realized what I had hoped for: blending healthy spirituality and sound principles of psychology pays off. I started to see significant healing in the lives of those coming to me for help with their depression and other emotional disorders.

Unfortunately, I failed to recognize that depression had been stalking me through these years. It was biding its time, waiting for the right moment to strike. As I treated others, I neglected myself and my own needs. I created the kind of environment where serious depression can get a beachhead and launch a major assault.

In retrospect, I recognize where depression and I had a few near misses in my youth. During my years in the seminary, I would have an occasional period of time when I felt sad and listless, not, however, to the point of impairing my ability to function. Like everyone else, I labeled these as "bad days" and went on, giving them only passing notice. Looking back, these clearly were minor episodes of depression.

And so, long before that morning dawned in November 1990, I had clashed with depression and had won. I was oblivious to the fact, however, that depression can strike again and again. In fact, researchers have found that the majority of patients with depression suffer multiple episodes—an average of five in a lifetime. Unfortunately, each time depression strikes, it is usually more severe and debilitating.

What you don't know can hurt you—and hurt you badly. I would find that out for myself.

"Why Me?"

Most of us share a common curiosity about why things happen the way they do. We want to know and identify the driving forces behind events: the cause-and-effect relationships. "Why did this happen? Why did it happen to them—or to me?" We want to make sense of things, to comprehend and understand.

At the end of my ten-month struggle with major depression, I wanted to know why it had happened. Why me? What were the factors that allowed this illness to overpower and overwhelm me?

Looking back, I see three powerful forces converged to form a trigger mechanism that detonated the major depression I experienced. These same three factors impact everyone to a greater or lesser degree.

Trigger #1: Genetics

It isn't uncommon for a person to be born with a genetic predisposition to this particular illness. Studies show that the first-degree biological relatives of patients who are depressed are more than twice as likely to experience a depressive episode than those without a history of depression.

Female relatives of depressed persons have a one-in-three chance of depression, whereas male relatives have a one-in-six chance. These rates are double those found in relatives of persons without depression. Children whose mothers have experienced depression appear to have a higher rate of depression than children of mothers who are not depressed. One study done with depressed adults who had been adopted as children found a higher rate of depression in their biological parents, as compared to the parents who had adopted them.

For many of us, heredity plays a significant role in the depression we experience. A veteran psychiatrist who has treated thousands of people for depression shares this from his clinical experience: "I seldom see a person with major depression without discovering that someone else in the family—usually a close relative, such as a parent—has also suffered from the same illness.

"Heredity brings both blessings and curses," he adds. "Our genetic inheritance can enable us to write a magnificent symphony or design a breathtaking cathedral. Yet, at the same time, it can weaken us, even destroy us. Someone with extraordinary gifts and talents can be a diabetic at age fifteen or suffer from schizophrenia by age twenty-five, largely because of an inherited genetic package."

This professional's advice is coated with hope, however: "The truly amazing thing that I've seen over and over again is how people turn events that are disasters of major proportions—like having a child with Down syndrome or going blind at age ten—into acts of tremendous self-sacrifice and courage. The very thing that could destroy a person actually transforms that person into a living saint. As a Christian, I don't believe that is simply genetics at work. I believe it to be the grace of God."

If you or a relative suffer from depression, and you are

27

wondering about the influence of heredity, examine your personal history to see if depression "runs" in your family. This will mean asking a lot of questions, probing, exploring, and investigating to see if patterns of depression can be identified in family members, both the living as well as the deceased. Frame your questions carefully.

- Has anyone in our family ever had a nervous breakdown?
- Has anyone in our family been hospitalized for depression or anxiety?
- Are there family members who have attempted or actually committed suicide?
- Have any of our relatives been treated by a doctor or therapist for mental or emotional disorders?

If a family member has been treated for depression, try to find out what form the treatment took. Research shows that what works well for one depressed person often works equally well for another depressed person in the same family, especially if an anti-depressant medication has been used.

Get as much information as you can about the mental-health history of family members. Granted, you may run into problems if you are adopted and do not have access to data about your family or origin.

As you make your inquiries, remain sensitive to family members' hesitancy, embarrassment, or even shame over the presence of mental illness. There are those who consider the issue a skeleton in the closet, one they do not want dragged out even for other relatives who are suffering the same illness. When this attitude prevails, it can be difficult to locate the kind of information that may benefit both you and other family members.

Often, however, more than mere genetics is at work when depression strikes.

Trigger #2: Stress

We all live with stress, and for the most part, we cope. But when stress reaches a high level, it is transformed into distress—a potent force that batters and bruises us emotionally and leads us into psychological and physical burnout. Sadly, few are aware of this at the time.

When we live a dysfunctional lifestyle, the abnormal eventually becomes the norm. We experience our unhealthy, dysfunctional behavior as acceptable and appropriate. Seldom do we realize how sick we really are.

In contemporary psychological literature, stress is often referred to as the "hurry sickness." Shortly before I experienced a second episode of depression, I was caught by the "hurry sickness" and was oblivious to what was happening. I would hurry from one event to another, one town to another, one person to another. I would counsel, celebrate liturgy, write, lecture. Certainly, I was doing worthwhile things, but I was doing too much—far too much—while allowing no time for my own renewal.

Doctors frequently warn their patients about the dangers of burning the candle at both ends, but there is nothing they can do, no prescription they can order, that can cure it. We are the only ones who can make the decisions that ameliorate stress and bring about some self-healing. I knew that, of course, but ignored the wisdom. Instead, I resolutely pushed onward, oblivious to my needs and limitations. When we no longer have any boundaries to protect us, it is then that we usually become a victim of too much stress.

When people come to me for counseling and complain about being overstressed, my assessment of their condition includes questions like the following:

- Do you feel overwhelmed?
- Do you feel like you're no longer in control of your own life?
- Do you feel exhausted and burned out, even when you've had rest?
- Do you feel, at times, that life is not worth living?
- Are you constantly tense and anxious?
- Do you have panicky feelings, along with excessive worry and anxiety?
- Do you suffer insomnia, headaches, stomach disorders, or other physical problems usually associated with too much stress?
- Do you have a lot of unresolved conflict in your life?
- Are you able to express and dissipate your inner anger?
- Are you a happy or an unhappy person?

Stress is exacerbated by such factors as low self-esteem, money or work concerns, relationship problems, psychological conflicts, and major life changes.

By the fall of 1990, I was emotionally exhausted and weary to the very core of my being. I was burned out and badly needed both rest and renewal—but I ignored these needs. I forged onward. When the final vulnerability factor manifested itself, it combined with my family history of depression and my stressed-out condition to push me over the edge into full-blown depression.

Trigger #3: Grief

The final component of this dark, unholy trinity is the universal human experience of grief. When we lose something or someone we value, we grieve. A child cries for weeks when his or her dog dies; when a home is destroyed, a family is plunged into profound grieving. Retirement, the end of one's working years, can make a person no longer want to live. That's grief—a normal and healthy reaction to loss. Loss, grief, and loneliness are all interconnected and make the pain even more unbearable at times.

There are different kinds and degrees of both grief and loss. For example, there are high- and low-grief experiences. A high-grief experience is an extremely intense reaction to a major loss, such as parents losing a child. A low-grief experience is less intense: the loss of a job that brought little satisfaction, for example. In general, the higher the level of attachment to someone or something, the greater the grief when that person or thing is lost.

There are also different kinds of losses. An accidental loss takes place unexpectedly: an automobile accident, for example. A developmental loss is more predictable, such as the death of aging parents, the moving away of adult children, and our own failing health as we age. There are individual losses that affect only an individual; there are collective losses that affect an entire family, community, or nation.

In the fall of 1990, I experienced two major individual losses that converged to create a high-grief reaction. They would bring me to the final threshold of major depression.

First, I lost my job. While working in a Catholic counseling agency, I was also helping out in a parish. I found tremendous satisfaction in my work and realized a great measure of success, as my psychospiritual approach to therapy was, indeed, helping people experience peace, healing, and new wholeness. My theories about the effectiveness of blending a healthy spirituality with good psychological principles were being validated.

I felt good about myself and was affirmed by my work. I was a healer and rejoiced in what I was. I knew God was using my skills in that particular setting to help many people who otherwise would never come to a priest in a regular church setting.

Without warning, I was asked to take another job in the agency. The new job would eliminate any further contact with the people I had been serving. More significantly, it would deprive me of the opportunity to practice the kind of healing therapy I had so carefully developed.

Rather than accept these limitations, I left the agency. I went back into full-time parish work, all the while grieving the loss of my counseling work. I knew that an entire sector of needy people would no longer be touched in ways that would help them realize peace.

I was angry at the unfairness of what had happened, angry at the lack of vision in Church leadership. Couldn't they see what they were doing not only to me but to the many who would now be deprived of my help?

As the anger seethed, it turned into rage—but it had nowhere to go. It churned in the corners of my heart and mind, burrowing deeper and deeper. In those dark corners, it was gradually transformed into something toxic and destructive.

I might have coped with the loss of my job had Sandy not died.

Sandy and I were like sister and brother. We grew up together and became best friends and soul mates. When she died in a tragic accident in late October 1990, something inside of me died too.

Although my grieving was profound, it was extremely private.

No one knew the extent to which I was affected by Sandy's death. I recall a friend looking into my face several months after Sandy died and saying, "You look like you've just lost your best friend!" I had.

Others guessed that something was wrong, but I brushed off their concern: "I have some kind of virus; it'll pass; I'll be fine." I had no desire to talk to anyone. I just wanted to be alone with my pain.

My entire inner life was plunged into darkness as though a fuse inside of me had blown. The storm clouds gathered in my mind and spirit, warning of an approaching emotional hurricane, but I no longer had the energy to seek shelter. Nothing mattered; nothing. My soul seemed shattered like a pane of glass, and the jagged edges lacerated me.

As grief, the final threshold to depression, buried its teeth in me, I hurt. The emotional pain was far worse than any physical pain I had ever experienced. I saw no way to bring the pain to an end or even reduce it to a more tolerable level. I felt like hell!

I wrote the following poem on November 3, 1990, three days before the major depression struck:

O, my sister, I feel your dying in my bones
gnawed to the marrow by grief.
I am no longer happy in my skin.
I, too, have been ripped open by the fangs
of the snarling, blood-gorged creature, death.
I bleed now from unseen wounds.
I long to daub my face with mud
and stand on some lonely,
windswept hill far into the night,
hands raised in wailing from the deepest soul caverns,
crying for you, for me,

for all who have gone before and are yet to be.
I have become the last person on earth,
forced to watch my race die with you.
Empty-eyed I sit here, unable to stir the dying embers,
resigned to the yellow eyes watching from the dark.
Something greater than myself
will have to summon the dawn.

Yet, I continued to function. In fact, my work didn't seem affected at all. Although I dreaded the approaching holidays and winter months, I felt I could cope. After all, I was both a priest and a therapist. I was protected by a special sacrament and possessed exceptional therapy skills. I could handle things. In spite of the savage inner pain, I would get through even if it meant crawling along until I felt better. *Nothing lasts forever,* I told myself. *This will pass.*

It didn't.

In early November, I felt the dull pain inside me change into something acute and stabbing, demanding my full attention. Alarms began to go off inside me, but I tried to ignore them. When I went to bed on the night of November 5, I felt utterly broken and empty, hoping sleep would help. Instead, I crossed the border from whatever vestiges of emotional health I still possessed into an uncharted wasteland of serious depression.

Heredity, stress, and unresolved grief came together in a powerful alliance and struck with full force. At that point, it became impossible to ignore the emotional havoc that erupted inside me with volcanic force.

The next morning, I began my long struggle for survival.

When Faith Falters

The first casualty that resulted from the onslaught of major depression was my faith. It faltered. For a time, I thought it might fail altogether. I was surprised by this, yet I don't know why. After all, I had seen this happen to many other depressed persons, including priests.

A close priest-friend of mine who had a severe heart attack told me that during the recovery period, he experienced depression so deep that he wanted to die. In his darkness, he experienced a total absence of God. He could not pray—did not *want* to pray. He could not read Scripture, and for a time, he even stopped celebrating Mass. Today, he refers to that time as his "atheistic period." It was a spiritually dry season that seemed interminable. He acknowledges that it did pass, and he discovered, or rediscovered, the love of God.

I could only hope for the same.

Depression and Prayer

Depression takes away many appetites—including the desire to pray. It goes beyond a sense of God's absence; it goes beyond a feeling that God is distant or that something is not right in your relationship with God. More than that, God seems to disappear.

Prayer quickly becomes an exercise in futility. You feel like you're talking to yourself and no one's interested—not even God because, after all, God has vanished. The feelings of disconnection, isolation, and loneliness, common to depression, are intensified when you feel God is absent. Your soul aches as much as your mind and spirit.

I had just lost one close friend. Now the one Friend who was even closer to me than Sandy was also gone. I remember saying to myself in the midst of this agony, "If this isn't the dark night of the soul, nothing is."

One sleepless night, I wrote this poem of desperation:

I swim into myself through raging seas,
From secret storms.
God, I do not know what dark debris
Will wash ashore at some deserted place
From all these.
I only know I looked into the waters
And could not see you in my face.

When my faith faltered, I made a major mistake in not seeking a competent spiritual director. Ironically, I was a spiritual director myself guiding countless others through the same thing. Yet, when it came to my own journey, the chains of darkness would not let me reach out for help. Instead, I talked to myself, telling myself all the things I tell others in crisis, but it didn't work. The words sounded empty and hollow—a weak spiritual pep talk and nothing more.

The Power of Touch

Because I had no spiritual director, I was also deprived of the opportunity to have someone pray with and over me. Many times in ministering to depressed persons, I found the laying on of hands, in or out of the context of the sacrament of the anointing of the sick, especially effective in alleviating some of the inner pain.

The laying on of hands is efficacious beyond the power of prayer; it connects to the power of touch. Physical human contact soothes, calms, and restores. But seldom does one touch a priest beyond a handshake, a pat on the back, or a brief hug.

Yet, the person in the throes of depression is touch-starved; I was. I wanted to be ministered to and consoled through the laying on of hands, but my choice to fight the illness alone blocked that opportunity. Although the evidence that I could not spiritually guide and direct myself through this faith crisis was manifest, I ignored it. I had made my decision to weather this storm alone—as so many others do—and I was going to stick to it.

One thing did provide me spiritual solace: the Psalms. These ancient song lyrics, like some of today's song lyrics, captured much of what I was feeling inside. I could read some of my favorite Psalms and discover that the psalmist of ages ago knew the inner regions of my pain. Psalm 130:1-2, for example, expressed my desperate need for God to hear me: "Out of the depths I cry to you, O Lord; hear my voice! Let your ears be attentive to my voice in supplication." Psalm 28:1-2 expressed the fear I knew if God would not hear me: "I call to you O Lord. O my Rock, be not deaf to me, for if you heed me not, I become as one of those going down into the pit." Some of the wording in Psalm 25:1-2, 16-17 voiced the extent of my distress: "To you I lift up my soul, my God. In you I trust. Let me not be put to shame; let not my enemies exult over me....Look toward me and have pity on me, for I am alone and afflicted. Relieve the trouble of my heart and bring me out of distress."

I recall one of my Scripture professors in the seminary, a man who had struggled heroically against alcoholism and won, saying that the Psalms provide a better study in human emotions than anything we will find in the writings of Freud. He was right. I knew Freud's writings, and they did nothing for me during this time of crisis. The Psalms did.

Little else was a spiritual help during this ten-month period of major depression. I continued to celebrate Mass, but the absence of God haunted my every word and action; reception of the Eucharist brought me little peace and consolation.

Strength in Weakness

Despite my own spiritual desert, my lifeless soul, and my savage darkness, spiritual power continued to flow out of me through the ordinary things that priests do.

A woman came to me for counseling on one of my worst days—a day I questioned my own survival because of the inner pain. I listened to her pain and concerns, and at the end of the session, she asked me to pray with her.

I don't know where the words came from, but I managed to offer some kind of short prayer. She later told me that she was so moved by the prayer that it cemented her decision to take part in the parish RCIA program and be received into the Catholic Church.

One night, as I tossed with sleeplessness, the telephone rang. A nurse at the hospital was calling to request baptism for a dying baby. I hurried to the hospital to find two frantic parents and a limp, nearly lifeless ten-month-old boy. As I baptized the baby with a thimbleful of water, the child began to scream—and breathe. Within minutes, color returned to his fair skin as he continued to breathe normally.

All of us in the room believed we had witnessed a miracle. The parents were grateful beyond words, and today the mother refers to her son as her "miracle" child.

During the heart of my depression, I preached a homily on hope—undoubtedly talking to myself. No one needed to hear about hope more than me! A week later, however, an elderly man told me that the homily had saved his life.

He had come to church that morning intending to receive Communion and then end his life. He felt he had nothing to live for. Somehow the homily touched his mind and heart, and he made a commitment not to give up or give in to despair. He chose, instead, to spend his remaining earthly life serving God more diligently than ever. Today, that man takes Communion to several nursing homes and offers encouragement to lonely, broken persons who often despair of hope, just as he did.

Review your own situation, and notice your own miracles. Although the dark night rages through the chambers of the soul, God's work continues. While we are at our weakest, our power to channel grace to others is not diminished. We often believe that we have to be at our best to effectively serve God. Yet, God uses us—and uses us well—even during the worst times of our lives, when we can't even minister to ourselves, much less others.

As Saint Paul tells us, there is a tremendous spiritual strength that comes from being weak. Letting go and letting God work, works. When we invite God to use us and our gifts, count on it:

God will. God does not wait until we are high-functioning or perfectly in control of our lives. God uses us just the way we are, even when we are not the way we think we should be.

God's Presence in the Absence

Depression possesses enormous power to affect every aspect of our lives, including our spiritual life. It causes a kind of "spiritual cataract" to form over the eyes of faith. This cataract obscures and distorts our vision of God and dims our awareness of God's presence in day-to-day life. We lose sight of God—but God does not lose sight of us. As Psalm 139 puts it: "For you darkness is not dark, and night shines as the day. Darkness and light are the same" (v. 12).

At the end of ten months, when the depression had finally lifted, I discovered that God had been with me all along. The silence of God did not mean *absence*. Rather, the silence was only my own space; God remained everything God is: love.

In the depression counseling I do today, I focus on this feeling of God's absence, this sense of separation from God; it is an important dimension of the healing process. When we acknowledge and accept the experience of God's distance, rather than fighting it or beating ourselves up because of it, we loosen the grip of fear and despair. We admit our darkness, and in that space, God's grace can enter.

When depression strikes, the Christian will experience an arid, desiccated faith devoid of spiritual feeling or any sense of closeness to God. It is frightening to the core of one's being to experience God as gone. When faith ceases to be life-giving, the whole universe becomes a meaningless black hole, empty of all purpose.

Those of us who suffer from major depression experience our faith as faltering. This is one of the features of a serious illness that characteristically disrupts every aspect of our existence. Reality is, however, that our faith does not fail. Spiritual equilibrium and peace will return.

Nothing is safe from depression, not even the soul. And when the soul is plunged into darkness, all the lights of joy and peace seem to have gone out—as indeed they have.

The Spiritual Consequences of Depression

As a whole-body illness, there are spiritual consequences to depression. In some ways, the spiritual aspects are the most dangerous to our well-being. When we lose contact with God, we feel truly alone, and despair can become more inviting, death, more appealing.

Yet, in that desolate space, in that desert, God roams. Our foremothers and forefathers in faith have taught us this. There, where we are stripped naked—even of hope—God's grace abounds. Some power greater than ourselves waits there and enables us to hang on, if only by our fingertips.

God's grace proved sufficient in the face of my own insufficiency. I lost my ability to find God, but God walked with me all along the way. Yes, my faith faltered, but God's saving grace, as a result, had a lot of room in which to work.

"Lord, I Just Want to Die!"

An immediate and overwhelming sense of doom and darkness greeted me that November morning. I knew something was wrong. The darkness of that fall morning had somehow managed to penetrate my mind and spirit. I knew instantly that major depression had struck with a vengeance and that I was in serious trouble.

What to do? I had a million things to attend to that day. Should I cancel everything and take a sick day? "No. I can manage. It'll be like going to work with the flu—and I've done that many times."

But brushing my teeth, shaving and showering, getting dressed, moving from one room to the next—it all took monumental amounts of energy. All I wanted to do was climb back into bed, pull the covers over my head, and sleep. At least sleep would allow me to escape the emotional pain. Yet, I knew that the cluster of anxiety bombs exploding inside of me would never let me sleep. I summoned all my strength and lurched into the day.

Incredibly, I survived the day and actually did well. I didn't miss any appointments and must have appeared to function normally. Only one person, an astute secretary, asked me if something was wrong; I told her no. "Well, your eyes look strange," she said. Several months later, this caring secretary admitted that she knew I was depressed but didn't know how to address the issue.

That evening, my attempts to relax were aggravated by restlessness. A heavy sense of sadness began to overshadow me, and within a short time, I began to sob. Not just cry, but sob. Tissues proved inadequate to absorb the tears, so I used a towel instead—then another and another.

I was startled. I had never cried this way before, yet there was absolutely no way to stop. The inexhaustible supply of tears demanded release. I had heard some of my clients explain that they could not control their crying, that the crying controlled them. In those moments, I knew their experience.

Sheer exhaustion brought an end to the sobbing after two hours. My eyes were red and puffy—and finally, I was tired. Still, sleep would not bless me. The restlessness remained.

I took a mild tranquilizer that my doctor had prescribed for occasional insomnia and found a few hours of escape sleep. By two o'clock, however, I was awake again—for the rest of the night. Time hung heavy as I tread through the hours "ruminating." My mind was invaded by persistent thoughts: I relived mistakes and failures from years past, mourned errors in judgment and bad decisions, and entertained hours of negative, self-defeating thoughts. Certain thoughts actually brought physical pain.

This first full day and night of major depression would be typical of many days and nights to come.

Ruminating Through Depression

The word *ruminate* means "to chew the cud," an activity of cows. Rumination is characteristic of depressed persons. They obsessively think and rethink the same thoughts over and over again.

Depression is a consummate deceiver. Through the rumination process, the depressed person begins to believe things about his or her life that are not true. Depression convinces a person that he or she is a total failure, worthless and unlovable. Consequently, the depressed person questions the very core purpose of life and the value of remaining alive.

Self-esteem is a major casualty of depression, and indeed, this was the case with me. Shortly after the onset of major depression, I began to believe in my own worthlessness: "I am a complete, abject failure. I've hurt others; I've failed those who depended on me."

Other Symptoms of Depression

Ruminating is only one major symptom of depression. Others include sleeping disorders, decreased or increased appetite with accompanying weight changes, poor concentration skills, inability to find pleasure or satisfaction in ordinary activities, persistent sadness, and recurring thoughts of death. Each symptom is worth examining.

Sleeping disorders: Disturbed sleep patterns become a routine part of life for the person experiencing depression. He or she may fall asleep with or without the aid of medication, awake a short time later, and remain awake the rest of the night—usually ruminating.

It isn't uncommon, however, for the person to actually *feel good* from the lack of sleep. In fact, sleep deprivation is sometimes effectively used in the treatment of depression. A lack of sleep that results in a sense of feeling good is one way to control the persistent sadness.

Decreased or increased appetite with accompanying weight changes: Throughout the stages of depression, facing mealtime can be a major ordeal. The person experiencing depression may eat a few bites and then push away the plate, or may eat three times the amount he or she normally would. It isn't unusual for the person to work hard at eating a decent meal only to vomit a short time later. In my own experience, our rectory cook began to think I was giving her a message about her cooking and wondered if she should start looking for another job.

With the loss of appetite, of course, follows a loss of weight. In two months, I lost more than fifteen pounds. When parishioners started noticing the weight loss, I explained it as a lingering flu bug: "And isn't it nasty what the flu can do to you!" They believed me.

Poor concentration skills: Even persons with sharp recall abilities will experience poor concentration skills when in the throes of depression. Both the victim and those who know the victim well will likely attribute the inability to concentrate to fatigue, overwork, age—anything but the grip of depression.

Some people did notice that I seemed distracted and confused and had difficulty concentrating, but they attributed it to overwork and exhaustion—and I was glad for that excuse myself. I have a superb memory, yet one day during a counseling session, I could not recall the name of the person I was counseling. I covered myself by mumbling something about fatigue.

When I read the wrong gospel, I made a joke of my mistake during the homily. Fortunately, the congregation focused on the humor and forgot about the mistake. Some days I would forget where I had parked my car. With nervous laughter, I would blame these memory lapses on old age—and as usual, people would laugh with me. No one guessed the link to depression because I continued to hide it so well.

Inability to find pleasure or satisfaction in ordinary activities: Movies, family gatherings, hobbies, reading, letter-writing, exercising: all routine activities become of little significance. The person experiencing depression finds little satisfaction in anything. Also, the person harbors a fear that he or she will have an inappropriate emotional reaction in an unguarded moment. These two factors combine to make simple daily living a nightmare.

I stopped reading novels: one of my all-time favorite activities. Some days I couldn't even bring myself to read the morning newspaper—my favorite way to relax over breakfast.

Persistent sadness: When psychiatrists or psychologists speak of mood, they're talking about a particular mental state, a sustained pattern of emotions, that affects and colors one's outlook on life and perception of reality. Mood can run the gamut from anger to elation.

Depression is called a "mood disorder." When depression sets in, a person's mood is upset. He or she becomes melancholic, which is to say, extremely sad.

If there were a Richter scale for sadness, I would have been at the far end of it. Never have I known sadness so heavy, so painful. I felt sad to the very marrow of my bones. Even when the other symptoms began to abate, the sadness remained.

At times, I actually felt the sadness, as though it were a physical reality. A woman describing the pain she experienced following her husband's death said that her heart felt like it was wrapped in barbed wire. That image is strong in the experience of depression. Sadness is not some emotion centered exclusively in the psyche. No, the sadness of depression is much more than that; it affects the entire body. The sadness is felt as sharply and causes as much pain as a ruptured appendix—maybe more.

Sadness in a depressed person may manifest itself in tears. If the tears are not fought, crying can actually be soothing and therapeutic.

In the early days of the depression I experienced, I was grateful that I could cry. The crying provided me a method of release and relief that drained some of the intense melancholic feelings. Because the sadness was worse at the end of the day, I would go to my room, where crying was safe. Although two other priests lived with me in the rectory, neither noticed I was having a problem—or if they noticed, they never mentioned it to me.

The person experiencing depression will become further distressed if the crying becomes unpredictable and uncontrollable. Outbursts of tears can happen anywhere: at the mall, at the gas station, at work. I would cry at department stores, restaurants, hospitals, doctors' offices. If anyone looked at me curiously, I would blow my nose, smile, and say, "Allergies." They would nod understandingly and not give me a second thought.

What was the meaning of all this? Was I, in fact, attempting to let others know that I was in pain? Was I tired of suffering in silence?

Perhaps. Ironically, no one really seemed to notice or care. People simply do not expect to see tears in the eyes of a priest. When they do, few will ask Father, "Why?" If subconsciously I was using the tears to get attention, it did not work.

As the crying continues, intensifies, and begins to explode in public, the person experiencing depression knows that the situation is worsening. The irony here is that sleep patterns may actually improve and an appetite may return, causing the person to think that recovery is occurring. Not so if the thought of death begins to dominate the person's thinking.

Recurring thoughts of death: A person suffering from major depression experiences recurring thoughts of dying. Some ruminate about ending it all by committing suicide, but never develop any sort of suicidal plan. Some depressed persons, however, are high on the lethality scale. They not only think about suicide, they actually put together a specific plan for self-destruction.

Far and away, suicide and suicidal attempts represent the most serious complication associated with major depression. Each year, fifteen percent of those treated for serious depression, even if they have been hospitalized, will commit suicide.

As I grew weary, so very weary, of fighting the depression and at the same time trying to keep my life together, death began to look like a sweet solution for such a monumental problem. At first, I had only vague and fleeting thoughts about dying. I would think about how wonderful it would be to leave this vale of tears, having finished my life's work, and go on to the fullness of the kingdom of heaven, where I could experience the perfection of joy. That sure beat being depressed here on earth.

Gradually, my desire to die grew stronger, and I began to take the idea seriously. I would entertain, in detail, thoughts such as "accidentally" crashing my car. Usually, I would put a mental block to my thinking by concentrating on life as God's most precious gift—although even this was purely an academic exercise.

Many persons, priests included, are not able to refocus their thinking, and thoughts of death become more real than fantasy. Eventually, these victims of depression are devoured by the darkness; they take their own life. What actually kills them, however, is the illness called depression—as sure as if they had died of cancer or pneumonia. Depression kills. I knew that. I also knew that I didn't want it to kill me. Up to this point, I was a victim of depression; I was determined not to be a casualty.

It was not that I was suicidal. I was not going to deliberately take my life. Yet, slowly but surely, the depression was squeezing the life out of me. My mind and spirit were dying and that was affecting my body. Eventually, the end result might prove to be the same.

I could feel my death desire growing. Many times before falling asleep, I would pray for death to claim me in the night: "Father, into your hands I commend my spirit for this night, asking you to take me home to you. I'm ready anytime you are, Lord." I had often witnessed the very same attitude in terminally ill and aging patients. It was an inner conviction that life had nothing more to offer, and they had nothing more to give, so why not move forward into eternity.

I had grown tired of living; it was time to die. One night, sleepless and desolate, I wrote this poem:

Woundedwandering, fog-filled,
I slip and stumble on sharp rocks
    slimy with despair.
I am bruised and bleeding,
    heart-hurt, soul-sore.
I can go no farther.
I await the sonrise,
    when the lonelylost are found,
And fanged fog flees from healing hope.
Maranatha!

The Beginning of the Beginning

I knew that I could not continue. The inner pain was wearing me down: depression was winning. I felt I was on the eve of destruction, yet I did not know what to do or where to turn. That too—that sense of being paralyzed—is a manifestation of the power of depression.

One night, about three months after the illness took hold of me, I prayed with unusual desperation for God's help. Scarcely had I finished my plea when the telephone rang. It was Father Dennis, a classmate. After apologizing for not touching base with me for a long time, he asked, "Is everything okay, Andy?" He explained his sense of concern for me.

As usual, I hesitated, so determined was I to fight the demon alone. Then, I took one small step in the direction of sharing some of my pain, and an avalanche followed. For over an hour, Dennis listened quietly, patiently, lovingly. When I finally stopped, his only comment was, "I'll be there tomorrow."

Although Dennis has had none of my extensive training in psychology, he is a deeply spiritual person and an excellent priest. He has an ability to see things clearly and find solutions for the thorniest problems—often through prayer. He drove two hundred miles the following morning to bring me some obvious wisdom: "You're in deep trouble and you've got to seek help right away."

Of course, I knew he was right. My decision to fight the major depression on my own was not only proving catastrophic, it was unbelievably stupid! I would never have allowed a severely depressed person I was counseling to do the same thing. It was a dead-end approach to healing; it simply would not work.

Yet, I had resisted help. I berated myself for attempting to be my own therapist and my own savior. I recalled the old saying: "He who treats himself has a fool for a patient." Dennis' simple statement gave me the courage to act. God worked through Dennis to speak to me of love and life—and I was able to hear. I was ready to seek help. I had come apart; with the right kind of help and some hard work on my part, I would come together.

As Dennis left to return home, I picked up the telephone and called my doctor.

COMING TOGETHER

PART II

Asking for Help, Searching for Healing

When a person who is experiencing depression connects with a professional, he or she will be hospitalized and/or given a prescription for an antidepressant drug. Because of the variety of drugs and the unpredictable side effects, prescriptions are often hit or miss at first.

Within forty-eight hours, I had told my doctor the entire story. His concern was evident. "Do you want to be hospitalized?" he asked.

No. I was functioning reasonably well, and hospitalization at a small general hospital in our community would have done little good. Because many of my parishioners were employed at the hospital, I would have spent more time fending off their well-meaning concerns and many questions than I would have spent recovering.

My doctor understood. "Nonetheless, you need to start taking some antidepressant medication right away. In fact," he scolded, "you should have been on something three months ago. I don't know why you waited so long to call me." I remained quiet—because he was, of course, right.

Because of my dry-mouth experience with one of the older antidepressant drugs, he chose a different one. It wasn't one of the new antidepressant drugs that had been much talked about in the news. This medication has been around awhile and has a good track record. It not only helps ameliorate the depression, it also has a sedative effect that helps the patient sleep.

It seemed like a good choice. I knew of others who had taken the medication with promising results. In fact, some report that they were able to identify the very moment the medicine began to work: "I was just sitting at my kitchen table when suddenly the mental fog lifted, and I felt free." "It was as though someone threw open every window in the house and let the light in."

A friend of mine, also a priest, shared his experience with this particular antidepressant. He had been standing in the living room of his rectory when suddenly he no longer felt sad. Instead, for the first time in years, he felt alive and happy. "The black cloud that had hung over my head for years disappeared. It was like a miracle," he remembers.

Unfortunately, the medication offered me no miracle.

Generally, with an antidepressant, the person begins to feel some effect in about a month. Because it takes such a long time to work, many persons get discouraged and stop taking it because they think it is ineffective.

I managed to stay on the medicine for ten days, increasing the dosage gradually, as the doctor had instructed me. Although the medication helped me sleep—sometimes eight hours a night—I struggled with side effects during the day. One of the side effects of this particular drug is agitation and heightened anxiety. I experienced both.

The anxiety I felt before I started the medication was greatly exacerbated. In addition to that, I became hyperactive. I could sit, uncomfortably at best, for a few minutes, then I just had to stand up and move around. I felt compelled to keep moving all the time.

Finding the Right Medication

Under the care of my doctor, I actually felt worse. I knew what was happening: I was unable to successfully tolerate the medication. After further consultation with my physician, I discontinued the drug. Within a day or so, the agitation stopped and the anxiety level lowered.

Fortunately, neither my doctor nor I was discouraged. Both of us had seen this kind of intolerance to antidepressants in our patients. It was simply a matter or exploring alternative medications.

Next, my doctor selected a new drug, one that had been receiving both favorable and unfavorable publicity. It was a "convenient" drug; I took it only once a day. Its main side effect was insomnia.

Gone was the sedative effect the other drug provided. Instead, I experienced difficulty getting to sleep. Once again, with my doctor's permission, I occasionally used a mild tranquilizer.

Nonetheless, this drug was far easier to tolerate, and I continued to take it daily. My soaring energy was one of the first indications that I had found a drug that would work for me.

I returned to my routine fifteen-hour workday with ease. In fact, I was practically manic at times.

The Limits of Medication

Although medication is one of the primary means of treating depression, it has its limits. There are dimensions of the disease that the medication sometimes does not alter: the sadness, the despair and the desire to die, for example. That's why even with medication many patients simply give up and give in to the full force of the illness, choosing some form of self-destruction. This may be a choice that is immediate and permanent, such as suicide, or something long-term (yet equally damaging), such as excessive alcohol consumption.

Unfortunately, depression tends to feed on itself. It breeds discouragement, which in turn exacerbates the depression. The combination of these two essential components of helplessness and hopelessness is kept alive and active as the illness runs its course.

Although the drug I took energized me and helped me function well, I was not deceived by what was happening. I knew that major features of my depression, the deep sadness and desire to die, were not being touched by the medication.

On one level, I was improving. On a deeper level, however, I was still continuing to deteriorate. Because I knew I was not out of the woods, I continued to report to my doctor. During the course of one conversation, he suggested that I get away from the parish for a while; I agreed.

I joined some friends on a short trip into Canada. My appetite had greatly improved, so eating was a pleasant experience, and the company of my friends was renewing and relaxing. Yet, I felt fragile and disconnected. I continued to hurt inside, and alone in my hotel room, I would often sob. Although the dark grip of the illness no longer brought me stabbing emotional pain, it continued to haunt me with a dull, exhausting ache.

During this time, I visited a young priest who had been diagnosed as having manic depression. For years, he had been experiencing many of the symptoms of major depression, but then his mood would swing to the opposite extreme. He would become excessively hyper, with unlimited energy and little need for sleep.

The rapid, unpredictable emotional changes he experienced were destroying him. When he started talking about taking his own life, several friends decided to intervene. They got him hospitalized, and while in a psychiatric unit, a psychiatrist diagnosed him as being manic depressive. He was placed on the drug lithium—and his entire life was transformed.

"I felt like I had been re-created," he told me. "So many times I just wanted to give up and end it all, but something kept me going. I believe with all of my heart that, deep inside of me, the still, small voice of God was encouraging me, telling me that I would be given a solution.

"There were a lot of days when I felt I was at the end of my rope, but somehow I managed to tie a knot and hang on. People who are depressed need a lot of support and encouragement. We just can't get well all by ourselves, yet we're usually so ashamed of being depressed that we don't ask for help in time."

He looked at me and saw the discouragement in my eyes. "Don't give up, Andy," he encouraged me. "Keep knocking on doors until the right one opens for you, as it did for me. And I'll pray that the door opens soon."

Beware the Seasons

Many depressed persons have more difficulty coping in the spring than through the long, gloomy months of winter. The highest suicide rates in the country, in fact, are not around the holidays or during the wintertime, as most people believe. Instead, the majority of suicides take place during March, April, and May.

Experts are not entirely certain why spring is the peak season for suicide. Perhaps spring brings about certain kinds of subtle physiological changes in our bodies that affect behavior. More probable, however, is that spring brings not relief but greater darkness to those already overwhelmed by stress. The dark winter days actually match the mood of the depressed person more than the sunny days of spring. Crawling back into bed on a cold winter day, for example, simply seems more natural, perhaps excusable, than "wasting" a beautiful spring day by staying in bed. Winter seems to accommodate the dark moods of depression more than spring, and in that way, it may actually provide a time of great comfort and safety.

For those who feel barely alive emotionally, spring brings not the promise of new life and new hope, but a stress-filled challenge that in their desperate struggle to survive, they interpret as the final straw. What little coping ability they have left becomes totally depleted in the bright light of spring; despair takes over and death is a welcome friend.

Beyond Medication

I knew that suicide was not an issue for me. I valued life. But this chronic, unending, daily experience of depression was wearing me down and making me feel lifeless. I so badly wanted to return to the land of the living.

The sadness persisted, as did the desire to die. Prayer continued to bring little peace, while my inner life remained a parched earth longing for rain. My doctor suggested that I look for a therapist so I could supplement the medication with talk therapy. I agreed but could find no one in our rural diocese who was experienced in working with depressed clergy.

Priests and clergy are hypersensitive about whom they see. Ordinary mental-health professionals sometimes lack the background necessary to work effectively with clergy. A Lutheran pastor once told me that after trying several therapists in the area, with little success, he connected with a doctor two hundred miles away who understood clergy issues. It made perfect sense to me, but driving long distances was too impractical, so I kept looking.

And the sadness continued to crush me. I would literally feel it coming on, almost the way some people sense an approaching storm. When it would finally strike, I would be overwhelmed by deep melancholy, and the tears would flow freely.

One day as I was leaving the hospital after having visited sick parishioners, a nurse said to me, "Father, you must be having a lot of funerals lately because you always look so sad." When I got to my car, I began to sob uncontrollably.

Something more had to be done—soon. I was losing the battle. I knew that—and I was frightened. I made an appointment to see my doctor, and we talked at length about what was happening.

With antidepressants, there are two problems: finding the right medication is only the first problem. Determining the right dosage can be equally perplexing. A thoroughly competent doctor may struggle for months to find the exact dosage for his or her patient—and all the while, the patient continues to suffer, even deteriorate.

There are professionals, however, who specialize in medication for diseases like depression: psychiatrists. That's what my doctor urgently recommended. "I can refer you to one," he offered, "but you've worked closely with a number of them in the treatment of your own parishioners and clients. You can see one of them if you like, but see someone, Andy, soon."

I knew Dr. Kirk was the professional I needed to see. Because he was a relatively young psychiatrist, he was on top of the latest treatment modalities and the variety of new drugs being developed by the pharmaceutical companies—drugs that were proving to be highly effective against a variety of mental disorders.

I was desperately hungry for healing, and by the very nature of his chosen profession, Dr. Kirk was a healer. I prayed that God would use him effectively.

The Doctor Is In

A variety of mental-health professionals are trained to treat mental disorders. They are often lumped together under the category of "psychotherapists." Although their training and methodalogies may vary, their objective is essentially the same: to assist persons recovering from mental/emotional dysfunctions so they can return to healthier, happier lives.

In this country, three professional groups spearhead the never-ending battle against mental illness.

Clinical social workers: These professionals are trained to diagnose psychological disorders and offer a variety of treatments from individual counseling to group therapy. They often assess the troubled person from the viewpoint of his or her interactions with the various community systems in which he or she lives.

Psychologists: Like clinical social workers, psychologists are also experts in human behavior. They, too, diagnose and treat mental disorders primarily through the use of talk therapy. They frequently utilize certain types of psychological testing to assist in assessing a patient's condition and aid in the treatment plan.

Psychiatrists: These professionals specialize in the treatment of the physiological or biological aspects of mental disorders. They are fully licensed medical doctors. Unlike social clinical workers and psychologists, these doctors are able to prescribe special drugs that have been proven effective in the treatment of these kinds of illnesses.

There continue to be many myths and misconceptions surrounding psychiatrists. For example, people commonly believe that someone going to a psychiatrist's office will be required to lie on a couch and tell everything about his or her life, going far back into childhood. In reality, this Freudian model of psychoanalysis is seldom used. Rather, psychiatrists spend more time making a determination about what kind of medication will quickly and effectively improve a patient's condition.

"Any person going to a psychiatrist must be crazy" is another myth that does tremendous damage to patients who are intimidated by this stereotype. The patients of many psychiatrists experience difficulty coping because of a chemical imbalance in their brain chemistry. They are not "crazy"; they are completely in touch with reality, but have trouble functioning well. With the right medication, their condition can be corrected or controlled.

If there is a chemical imbalance or some physical cause of a particular mental illness, no amount of psychotherapy is going to help the condition. One of my parishioners received nearly a solid year of psychotherapy with a psychologist, including group therapy, but only felt worse at the end of the year. She saw a psychiatrist who prescribed a drug which he thought would help, and within a month, she was functioning superbly and making plans for a new career.

One major advantage that psychiatrists have over other physicians is that they are specialists in the use of psychiatric medications. For example, a psychiatrist may combine one medication with another to make it even more effective in treating a mental disorder, whereas a doctor who is a general practitioner would probably not be trained in this technique.

Dr. Kirk listened carefully and took copious notes as I told him my story. When my voice cracked and tears filled my eyes, he could clearly see my extreme sadness. "You are still experiencing major depression, Andy, and what I find remarkable is the fact that you've been able to function so well while being so ill." I felt embarrassed, again, for having delayed my own recovery.

We talked about hospitalization, and both of us agreed that there was little point in being hospitalized in the psychiatric unit attached to the hospital with which he was affiliated. If hospitalization were warranted, a facility with experience in treating clergy was needed. There was, in fact, such a facility downstate, but I wanted to save that option as a last resort, especially if my condition deteriorated to the point where I could no longer function.

As we talked further, Dr. Kirk began to focus on some of the factors that contributed to and exacerbated my experience of depression. "You have a lot of unresolved anger that you need to process, Andy. It's not only unresolved, but clearly you have a hard time expressing anger in the first place. It stays unresolved—and, of course, contributes significantly to your depression." I agreed.

When a psychiatrist has pinpointed a contributing element such as repressed anger, for example, he or she will suggest that the patient seek psychotherapy with a psychologist. Using both approaches expedites recovery. While the psychiatrist continues to monitor the medication, changing both the type of medication and the dosage as needed, the psychologist works with the patient to develop skills for coping.

Persistence and Selectivity

The importance of finding the right drug and dosage cannot be overemphasized. Many persons struggling with depression become discouraged because the process of finding the right drug and the right dosage is so hit or miss. It isn't unusual for doctor and patient to explore as many as half a dozen different drugs and dosages before finding one that is effective and causes limited side effects. Persistence is a much needed virtue.

I felt confident that Dr. Kirk would work with me through this process. In the meantime, I began to consider psychotherapy. Working with a psychologist would give me a two-edged sword in the battle against depression. I felt good about that. Healing had to be just around the corner.

It wasn't.

Although the theory of applying both psychiatry and psychology to the struggle with depression is valid and effective, my initial attempts were frustrating. That is not to say that the theory is wanting; it isn't. Persistence remains crucial.

At first, increasing the medication seemed to help. My high energy level returned, and I did have several good weeks. Both Dr. Kirk and I were pleased. The higher dosage seemed to be the answer.

But then something changed. I could feel the sadness returning. The nights of tears resumed, and the icy desire not to live began to haunt me again. I knew I was loosing ground.

With the increased dosage of medication, I began to experience short-term memory losses. I could remember things that happened thirty years ago, but I couldn't remember my cousin's name, my father's phone number, or where I put my checkbook.

That side effect could have been tolerated if the medication had been effective with the other symptoms, but it was not. I was disappointed and frightened. Valuable time had been lost. I had to start over, giving whatever new drug we selected the necessary period to build up to a therapeutic dosage in my body. That would be a month to six weeks—perhaps more.

At about the same time, I realized that I had chosen the wrong psychotherapist for me—and I emphasize *for me*. He had impeccable credentials and many years of experience. I had chosen him primarily because he had counseled other priests; I valued that part of his professional background. After two sessions, however, I knew that we were not a good match.

Persons experiencing depression have to be selective about the therapist they work with. Credentials and experience are not sufficient criteria. The therapeutic relationship between a psychotherapist and a client is a mysterious entity. Often, it is the relationship itself that proves to be the healing factor, not so much what is discussed or explored. Because of that, it is crucial that the client have full confidence and trust in the therapist. If the person suffering depression does not experience a tremendous confidence and comfort within three visits, he or she should talk with the therapist about these misgivings and consider another professional. It's the client's prerogative to interview a therapist to ascertain if the match is right. No one should walk into therapy assuming that a satisfying professional relationship is inevitable. If, in fact, the match is not good, much ground may be lost.

Another factor that affects the therapeutic relationship is the phenomenon of transference. The client can "transfer" or displace feelings or attitudes from prior significant relationships (parental, for example) on to the therapist. Positive transference takes place when the displaced feelings and attitudes are affection, warmth, and care. Negative transference includes feelings of hostility, rejection, or coldness. Most transference takes place at an unconscious level. If there is a high level of emotional intensity present in the therapeutic relationship, some degree of transference is likely occurring.

I saw the psychologist twice; he seemed genuine, warm, gentle, and compassionate. However, I found him passive and nondirective. I soon realized that if I stayed with him, I could look forward to months of expensive therapy.

What I wanted, instead, was short-term therapy that would provide me with the focus and skills I needed to effectively combat the depression. I wanted to be empowered for self-healing. I did not want to spend a long period of time looking deep into my past for ghosts that might not even be there. I wasn't looking for a quick fix; I wasn't that naive. I simply did not have the luxury of time and finances to explore long-term therapy. I knew the value and power of short-term therapy because I was a practitioner of it myself with my own clients. I knew lasting results were possible—and that's what I wanted.

So, I was once again without a therapist. I was also in the process of working with Dr. Kirk to—once again—change my medication. Persistence.

Dr. Kirk recommended a relatively new drug to the market, one that was having a lot of positive results. Although this was an excellent medication, there was no guarantee that it would work for me. It would take at least a month to find out. We also discussed the fact that sometimes certain patients simply do not respond well to the class of drugs I was taking. If, after a sufficient trial-and-error period, these antidepressants proved ineffective, it would be time to switch to an entirely different type of drug called an MAO (monoamine oxidase) inhibitor. These had a history of working well in patients who have not responded to other kinds of drugs. The main drawback for the person taking MAO inhibitors is diet; certain kinds of foods can create adverse physical reactions that can be dangerous.

So, I started over again. Persistence.

I blessed the new medication and prayed that God would use it for healing. God can use anything and everything. For healing, God often uses the very ordinary things of our lives, such as medicine, relaxation, exercise, and proper nutrition.

I had no solutions of my own to offer at this point. I knew that I could not bring about my own recovery. I would have to depend upon the right medication and the right kind of therapy to facilitate healing, and I was trusting God to provide both. Somehow I aroused my weak, faltering faith and made a decision to let go and let God take over fully.

"I'll accept whatever solution you provide me, Lord," I remember praying. "Only please hurry!"

Something More

A good therapist will help the person experiencing depression talk about feelings and experiences. The therapist will raise questions that enable the client to search unexplored inner areas to make sense out of what is being shared. A good therapist will help the person set goals directed at identifying the psychological roots of depression and construct a road map that will lead to recovery. Eventually, the pieces of the painful and perplexing struggle with depression will begin to come together.

Two days after Dr. Kirk changed my medication, a counselor-friend mentioned a therapist he highly recommended. He commented on her private practice, her experience with treating clergy (in fact, she was the daughter of a clergy person), and her success with difficult cases; within fifteen minutes, I had an appointment with her. Three days later, I was sitting in her office.

With Dr. Martin, the floodgates opened. I began to pour out feelings I didn't know existed deep within my darker spaces. Dr. Martin was an excellent listener. She could ask questions that forced me to think. For days after an appointment, I would continue to process the specific issues we had discussed. Today, looking at my notes from those sessions, everything seems obvious; yet at the time, these realizations had enormous significance. Always the goal of good psychotherapy, my life was changing for the better.

The following steps indicate my healing process. I share them for the benefit of those who are struggling with depression. To expedite your own healing, ponder my list, make your own, and share it with a therapist. Your list will be different, of course, but nonetheless significant in your healing journey.

The number-one priority in my life has to be my recovery from depression. Everything else pales in comparison. The most important person in my life right now has to be me. This is not an attitude of selfishness. It is, in fact, a form of basic survival. Attending to my own basic needs is not selfishness and does not mean I'm becoming egocentric or self-centered. God wants me to take care of myself; God wants me to survive. Even Jesus took time away from his ministry for rest, relaxation, and prayer. I can and will do the same.

At this time, I am just as needy as the neediest person I am attempting to serve. My most basic need is to put time and effort into my own personal healing. This will mean letting others help me, just as I help so many in their own time of need. Now I must allow myself to be assisted by others. In no way is this a sign of weakness. I cannot heal alone or find the wholeness I seek in isolation or some kind of vacuum. God has created me to be a social creature. I am at my best when I minister to others while allowing them to minister to me in my own woundedness. It is not good for me to be alone, especially while I'm suffering.

I need to give myself permission to grieve fully and unashamedly for Sandy, for my mother, for my sister, and for any other major losses sustained throughout my life. Grieving is one of the most natural and normal things I can do. When it is denied or bottled up inside, grieving becomes impaired and dangerous to my well-being. Far better to grieve in a healthy way than to give in to sorrow so completely that I am destroyed.

I need to give myself permission to be angry. Anger, too, is a perfectly normal emotion and can be appropriate under certain circumstances. For example, it can energize me so that I can take action to change certain things for the better. If I swallow my anger and let it begin to grow inside of me, I create a demon that will eventually attempt to destroy me—and it will succeed if I let it. Anger transformed into rage truly is the killing emotion. I need to release my anger in the right proportions so that I can control it—so that it no longer controls me. I need to be honest about my anger—neither denying it nor feeding it in such a way that gives it a life of its own. Honesty with my anger also means a willingness to admit that sometimes I am angry at God. God is the one who gave me this emotion. If at times I direct it against God—well, God can handle it.

My unresolved grief and anger have something significant to do with my depression, even if there are other contributing biological and genetic factors at work. The ongoing depression tells me that both the grief and the anger have burrowed deep inside of me to create a world of their own—a world of darkness and despair.

With God's help and with the help of others, and drawing upon my own strength, I must make these dark forces unwelcome inside of me so that they leave me. I must deliberately choose to let the light in.

Because the mind puts great belief in what I say to myself, I must be far more careful with my self-talk. Negative and highly critical self-talk and self-evaluations will only feed the depression and make it worse. I need to work hard at eliminating the distorted, untrue self-talk and work at being more positive and self-affirming. The conversations I have with myself can slow down or speed up my healing. At least in part, it is true to say that I helped "think" my way into a state of depression. I can also choose to "think" my way out of it by making my internal dialogue less negative and bleak and far more positive and uplifting.

It is time to stop beating up on myself for real or imaginary failures. I am not perfect, and that is all right. God loves and accepts me just the way I am. I need to work at loving and accepting myself with all my weaknesses and flaws. I am a good person, and I must learn to fully respect myself and treat myself as a good person. This means being kind and gentle with myself—tolerating mistakes and failures in myself, just as I tolerate them in others. I can choose not to be my own worst enemy and instead be my very best friend. The choice is mine to make.

I am more than what I do; I am more than a priest. I am a valuable person in my own right. My worth comes not only from the things I do, no matter how significant they are, but from the fact that I am a child of God, created with inherent value and worth. Even if I were not a priest, I am someone of enormous value. Even if I were not a priest, God loves me as much as anyone. I need to see myself as valuable apart from what I do, for I am much more than what I do.

Because I have value as a person, I do not have to keep trying to validate my self-worth through my workaholic tendencies. Work can be as addictive as any drug. Workaholism will only prove to be destructive and ultimately self-defeating. If I am exhausted and burned out, I will stay depressed and anxious. The feeling that I am not accomplishing enough does not mean I have to be more and more active. Less is more; small is beautiful. A one-track life based only on my work is an anemic, empty life at best. I need to strive to develop a more normal, healthier lifestyle that allows for a variety of experiences, not just work. I must avoid compulsively transforming my work into my master or another god, lest I become enslaved by what I do. If I try, I can modify my behavior related to my work so that it becomes more refreshing and pleasurable, less exhausting and debilitating.

I need to avoid saviorism—the desire to always be a rescuer and save others from their problematic situations. Saviorism presumes that I know what is best for others and that I possess the solutions for their problems. Often, this is simply not the case, and I need to realize my limitations. I am not privy to some kind of master plan that allows me to change others and transform their lives for the better. I am not the Messiah. I am a weak, fragile human being just like everyone else. I must allow others to make choices, even if they appear to be bad ones. It is by their own choice making that people grow and mature as human beings. I can be an instrument and channel of God's grace and healing, but saving people is the exclusive domain of God. God is the only one who saves; I need to let God work at saving and transforming me, instead of trying to play God myself—for myself and others.

I need to acknowledge that I have some control in some areas, but that I cannot possibly control everything and everyone— and shouldn't even try. I need to work at letting go and letting God manage my life and the lives of those who touch mine. By being less controlling, I can find greater serenity and peace. Being less controlling is another avenue to recovery because it makes me aware of the fact that the management of the universe does not depend upon me. Increasingly, I need to turn persons and situations over to God and not try to manipulate them according to my own blueprint.

I need more companionship and less isolation. I need to have the feeling of being connected to others. I need more intimacy— intimacy in the broadest sense of being close to another. I must work at developing and expanding my friendships to reduce the impact of loneliness in my life. For me, loneliness is a significant source of stress that is damaging to my health. I don't have to be—and don't want to be—a "lone ranger" anymore. My friends and their friendship can help reduce my depression and greatly enrich the quality of my life and my work.

I need to stop being so hard on myself. There is no need to drive myself unmercifully and unrelentingly. I am much too overcommitted and overextended. It is all right to cut back, to slow down, and to say no. Spending all my waking hours pleasing others while neglecting my own basic needs is harmful and wrong. It makes me feel like a puppet, which then causes me to become angry, and that anger manifests itself as depression. By being less hard on myself, I will experience less depression. Healthy self-love means learning to be kind to myself, more tolerant, and self-accepting. Resolving these issues is absolutely crucial to my well-being.

A Holistic Approach to Therapy

With a list of this nature, the person struggling with depression is ready to do the hard work required in therapy—as well as the hard work done outside of therapy. These core issues help the person address and process issues that medication cannot touch. In addition to working with Dr. Martin on these issues in her office, I spent hours journaling with them on my own. Journaling, in fact, became a form of therapy.

Dr. Martin believed in a holistic approach to healing, to which I eagerly responded. I needed healing in mind, body, and spirit, and I was delighted that her therapeutic approach integrated all three. She urged me to exercise, so I became more conscientious about walking, usually twenty minutes a day. No matter how bad a day I was having, I felt better after a short walk. Shortly after I adopted the practice of walking, I found this quotation by the Danish philosopher Sören Kierkegaard:

> Above all, do not lose your desire to walk: every day I walk myself into a state of well-being and walk away from every illness; I have walked myself into my best thoughts, and I know of no thought so burdensome that one cannot walk away from it...but by sitting still, and the more one sits still, the closer one comes to feeling ill....Thus if one just keeps on walking, everything will be all right.

Dr. Martin and I also reviewed my nutritional patterns. I began to use more vitamins and tried to reduce caffeine consumption. Caffeine is strongly linked to feelings of anxiety and even panic attacks. Within a short time after reducing my caffeine intake, I began to feel less edgy.

In addition to walking and watching my nutrition, I started meditation exercises. Dr. Martin gave me material on meditation done in conjunction with the relaxation response of deep breathing. It is an effective way to eliminate stressful feelings and experience inner tranquillity. I would breathe in through my nose and exhale through my mouth until my mind and body were quiet and I felt calm inside. Then I would use a version of the Jesus Prayer in unison with the deep breathing: "Lord Jesus Christ, Son of the Living God, have mercy on me a sinner."

After fifteen minutes of meditation, I invariably experienced a sense of peace and well-being. I was praying again—praying and reconnecting with God. The combination of relaxation and meditation proved to be a potent medicine.

Finally, rounding out my holistic recovery program, Dr. Martin urged me to find a hobby or go back to an old one that I had once enjoyed. I had always wanted to improve my ability at the piano, but hadn't paid attention to it in years. Here was my chance. Within a short time, I found playing the piano not only relaxed and soothed me but also ministered to my mind and spirit. When I played the piano, I felt happy, like welcoming home an old friend who had been away for a long time.

I saw Dr. Martin over a period of three months—not a long time. After each session, I felt better. I began having more "good" days than "bad" days because something was happening inside of me. The psychotherapy combined with the antidepressant medication to affect me in positive ways. I experienced much less sadness and oppression, and inside of me, winter seemed to be melting; the warmth of spring seemed to be budding forth.

It was almost too good to be true, yet it was not my imagination; it was true. I was beginning to come together again. I could feel myself beginning to heal!

Happy Days Are Here Again!

The person recovering from depression will feel tremendous relief as medication and therapy work together in the healing process. Antidepressants and good therapy, however, do not eliminate problems, struggles, and difficulties from a person's life. Although the bad day is a myth when applied to depression, it is a fact of life nonetheless. People do, in fact, have bad days.

The person recovering from depression will still experience the normal things that all human beings experience. Struggles and bad days, however, are not menacing or overwhelming. Working through the difficulties is easier, less stressful, and more successful. Discouragement is momentary, and clear thinking for problem solving comes naturally. With the mind clear of the fog, simple, straightforward thinking becomes a joy.

With the fading of sadness, so goes the tears. Episodes of sobbing become fewer and less intense, until they fade completely from routine life. The person recovering from depression can begin to trust his or her emotions again, knowing that the tears are the right amount at the right time.

Morbid thoughts about death and leaving this pain-filled world to be with the Lord recede as well. Life, right here, right now, looks and feels good. Simple things become sweet: a rainbow, a child's laughter, a song on the radio. It feels good to be alive, literally. Recovering depressed persons are ready to live until they die, instead of feeling themselves die a little each day while longing for the final fulfillment of that agonizing process. They stop treating life as though it were a terminal illness and acknowledge it as the wonderful gift it is.

Praying Again

Perhaps the greatest surprise and best gift of all in my own recovery process was my ability to pray once again. The barriers between myself and God, which somehow the depression had so skillfully and effectively constructed, came crashing down. I felt God's presence again. It was like having your best friend, who's been away—far away—show up at your front door. There was so much to talk about, and I talked to God nonstop.

Just as I had used the Psalms during the arid time when I lost God and felt utterly forsaken, I used the Psalms to thank and praise God for the salvation experience that was so real to me during my recovery process. Over and over, I prayed two Psalms in particular that captured my joy. Hear the joy in these verses from Psalm 30: "I will extol you, O God, for you drew me clear and did not let my enemies rejoice over me. My God, I cried out to you and you healed me. You brought me up from the nether world; you preserved me from among those going down into the pit...You changed my mourning into dancing. You removed my sackcloth and clothed me with gladness so that my soul might sing praise to you without ceasing. Forever will I give you thanks, O God" (vv. 2-4, 12,13).

Hear the gratitude and relief expressed in these verses from Psalm 116: "I love the Lord because he has heard my voice in supplication, because he inclined his ear to me the day I called. The cords of death encompassed me, the snares of the nether world seized upon me; I fell into distress and sorrow, and called upon the name of the Lord: 'O Lord, save my life!'...I was brought low, and God saved me. Return, O my soul, to tranquillity, for God has been good to you. For he has freed my soul from death, my eyes from tears, my feet from stumbling. I will walk before the Lord in the land of the living" (vv. 1-4, 6-9).

And God, in turn, talked to me! Over and over again, I found myself pondering the same Scripture passage: Isaiah 43:1-4. "Fear not, for I have redeemed you. I have called you by name and you are mine. When you pass through the water, I will be with you; in the rivers you shall not drown. When you walk through fire, you shall not be burned; the flames shall not consume you. For I am your God, the Holy One of Israel, your savior.... You are precious in my eyes and glorious, and...I love you."

Each time I read these verses or heard them read aloud, it was like receiving a telegram from God. After feeling lost and abandoned for so long, the passage blessed me beyond anything I can express. I felt loved, affirmed, accepted by God—again. I felt found! I was home, safe.

What a Glorious Feeling

After the Masses on Labor Day weekend in 1991, I went to a friend's lakeside cottage to unwind and rest. I had steadily been feeling better, yet something continued to be wrong. The depression had ebbed, but it was still present. I continued to experience a dull emotional ache, like a bad tooth might produce.

I certainly was doing everything within my power to drive it completely from my life. I was seeing Dr. Martin and taking the antidepressant medication faithfully. Exercise and relaxation were a regular part of my daily routine. I felt I had turned a corner on depression and was healing, but completing the goal remained elusive. A certain nagging sense of sadness continued to haunt me. All my efforts to dislodge it had been in vain—until that weekend.

When I woke up that morning, I lay still for a moment. It was quiet, deeply quiet, except for the sound of loons calling to one another on the lake. In the stillness, I knew something was different, but I couldn't put my finger on it. I got up, made coffee, and went out on the deck overlooking the serene lake. There was hardly a ripple across its mirrorlike surface. The sun was rising over the water, turning the sky into a gorgeous palette of blue, red, gold, and orange. A bass jumped gracefully; the loons continued to chatter mysteriously. Life!

Suddenly, I felt like laughing—then I knew. It was gone; the sadness was gone. A scene from a movie came racing to my mind: Gene Kelly dancing in the rain and singing, "What a glorious feeling, I'm happy again."

I felt happy! Genuinely happy, even joyous. I felt free and whole—nine weeks to the day that I had begun to take the new medication, I felt happy. Beyond a shadow of a doubt, I knew that the new medication had begun to work with maximum effectiveness. The depression was gone.

At first, it seemed too good to be true. Would it last? The depression had been deep and seemingly interminable. Would the medication, psychotherapy, and other weapons from my therapeutic arsenal keep it away? Was I really healed?

I was optimistic but cautious. I ventured back into my life and work like a blind man gaining his sight. Everything seemed so bright and clear. After those long months of looking at the world through a dark haze, I was walking in the sunlight again. Life took on a technicolor quality. Gone were the gloomy, dark colors that coated everything during those ten months of depression.

It actually takes some getting used to, this being happy stuff, but it was wonderful! I not only felt good physically, I felt good mentally. The constant mental pain was gone, and in its place was a feeling of calm well-being. I felt safe.

In looking for an image that aptly describes what had happened to me, I find myself pondering the Lazarus story in John's Gospel. Lazarus underwent some kind of resurrection experience. So did I. One quiet morning I wrote this short poem.

Lazarus-like
>   limbs tied, limping
>   trembling from tomb-terror,
>   I lurch forth into light and life
>   squinting, stunned
>   stammering gratitude for death deliverance.
>   Attitude altered forever by Godgrace,
>   I dance delightedly into a new day.

A week passed; two weeks; a month; two months. I felt good. I saw Dr. Martin a few more times, then decided to stop psychotherapy. Dr. Martin was thoroughly delighted that I was feeling so strong, so steady.

Six months passed, then eight. There were no signs of depression. My energy level remained high, and I was functioning well. I accepted a new assignment from my bishop, relocating to a troubled parish for a period of four months. As it turned out, I did well in a setting that had been marked by strife. It was a badly divided parish, much in need of reconciliation and healing—and

I found myself rising to the challenge. If anything, I felt that my gifts as a healer had been strengthened by my experience with major depression.

Have I Been Healed?

To the person who has struggled with depression, the feeling of relief and new life can be intoxicating—and unsettling. One wonders, "Will this happen to me again? Should I stay on the medication?" The answers are not black and white.

If there is a depression-producing chemical imbalance in the brain that the medication counteracted, the person may have to remain on medication in some form for the rest of his or her life. It amounts to the same physiological situation as a diabetic taking insulin daily to control blood-sugar levels.

I continued to see Dr. Kirk every three months so he could renew my prescription and keep an eye on my progress. Knowing that the question of medication continued to be a concern—for both of us—we decided to experiment. I would try to wean myself from the medication; if I started having problems, we would try something else.

I reduced my dosage from three tablets a day to two tablets a day. After a week, I reduced the dosage further to one tablet a day. Finally, I discontinued the medication completely. Within a week of drug-free life, I noticed a difference. The sadness was back, and I was sobbing. My thinking was not as clear, and my concentration was less sharp. A low-grade kind of depression had set in. When I checked with Dr. Kirk, he instructed me to return to the full dosage: three tablets a day. He felt confident that I had endogenous depression: depression originating in the chemistry of the brain. Very likely, I'll remain on the drug for a long time, possibly the rest my life.

Have I been healed of depression?

Healed is not a word I would use, because my particular form of depression is connected to some chemical imbalance in my brain. It can surface again, especially if I fail to remain on the medication. Drawing on all the resources available to me, I am able to control it and control it well.

Will I become depressed in a major way again?

The possibility is always there. Relapses of depression are not uncommon. If I do become victim to the illness again, I will fight back with the same weapons I've found effective in the past: medication, psychotherapy, relaxation techniques, prayer, exercise—anything and everything that works. I did not rid myself of major depression by a single method. The depression was powerful, and it took a constellation of allies to drive it away. If I need to, I will use them all again—*sooner*!

Sharing Our Stories

More and more, I find myself sharing parts of my story with the depressed persons I counsel. Invariably, they are surprised.

"Father, you look so together, so in control of your life."

"Looks are deceiving," I tell them. A person only hours away from suicide may look as though he or she doesn't have a care in the world. We hide things well, usually to our detriment, not our credit.

When I share my story with someone who is depressed, the person seems to find hope. "If you got through it, maybe I can too" is a typical response.

I came apart, but I came back together. If you are struggling with depression, I urge you to get help quickly. If you know someone who is struggling with depression, support him or her;

encourage professional attention. I especially urge priests and clergy who read this book and are battling depression to find help. You are worth the time and money. You deserve recovery. The longer you wait, the harder it will be to treat the depression, and in fact, the depression will probably worsen. I waited too long; as a result, I was nearly destroyed. Don't do the same thing.

By the grace of God and with the help of others, those of us who come apart can make the journey back to wholeness and health. Start now. It is time to get better.

The Lessons of Depression

Illness can be a stern and demanding teacher. In the grip of illness, we often learn lessons far more valuable than those learned when life is easy and comfortable. "Pain," said C.S. Lewis, "is God's megaphone."

Illness gets our attention! It causes us to reexamine and re-align our priorities to focus on what's really important. Illness can force us to reevaluate our entire life. It gives us permission to say certain things and address certain needs that otherwise would remain ignored.

Educate Yourself About Depression

Depression teaches you that you don't know much about the illness itself. If you or someone you know suffers from depression, learn all you can about the illness and seek professional help. The following pointers will direct you in your efforts.

Depression is a treatable illness. It responds to a combination of psychotherapy and medication. If depression is not treated, however, it will probably worsen.

Do not treat depression unprofessionally. I possessed many

therapeutic skills, but was unable to treat my own depression. In fact, this approach significantly delayed my recovery.

If you have the mentality that says "I can fix this by myself" or someone you know has adopted this mind-set, the depression is going to cause serious damage. To get healthy, help is crucial. Isolation only makes depression worse, more dangerous.

Because the treatment modalities for depression, such as psychotherapy and/or medication, involve a certain amount of experimentation, it is easy for the person suffering from depression to become discouraged. As my story indicates, it took months to get the right therapy and antidepressant combination.

The temptation, however, is to think that nothing is working—so why bother! Yet, the very nature of the illness of depression is such that a person becomes easily discouraged. Remember: depression lies! Don't listen to it. Recovery is possible—*likely*.

A major factor that inhibits depressed persons from seeking help is a certain sense of shame. The experience of shame says, "There is something wrong with me. I am flawed, unlovable, and no good. I deserve bad things; I deserve to be sick." Unfortunately, this sense of shame can block treatment while continuing to feed the depression. For many, depression is a humiliating illness to be kept hidden from others, which means continuing to suffer in silence.

Depression contains a message for our lives. Depression is a mood disorder that alerts us to areas of chaos in our lives. Wise people heed the message and use it to help change those areas where attention is needed. The experience of depression is an opportunity for growth when viewed with this perception.

My depression gave me some strong messages—messages that I did not want to hear. Depression would not let me ignore the fact any longer: my life was out of control. Stress was battering me, grief was drowning me, and many of my deepest needs were being ignored. The depression broke down my denial to where I could no longer run from myself. Although the illness could have killed me, it actually became a gift. It forced me to look at my life honestly and make decisions for my own well-being. Had it not been for the struggle with depression, I would not have done either.

Depression can bring death; often it does. But it can also bring an end to some self-defeating and self-destructive behaviors that are damaging us more than we may realize. If we listen closely to the voice of depression, it will speak to us of life.

There is a link between our thinking and our depression. The Chinese have a saying: "Our thoughts can kill us." I believe that's true. We talk to ourselves all the time, and far too often our inner dialogue is self-critical and negative. The bleak, negative statements that we make about and to ourselves eventually start to erode our self-esteem, just as persistent drops of water erode a rock.

A few months ago, I went through a difficult week; my thinking once again became negative. During that week, I had a vivid dream; I dreamed I was feeding chunks of meat to a large black dog, and the dog was devouring the meat ravenously. When I woke up, I immediately understood the significance of the dream. The black dog represented depression, and I was feeding the depression with my thoughts, outlook, attitudes, and interpretations. In effect, I was inviting the depression back into my life.

That day I began to transform my self-talk into affirmatives: statements and thoughts that build up and heal. It was hard work—remains hard work—but if I monitor my thinking, I can do it.

Faith alone is not enough to fight depression. As believers, we trust in the power of our spiritual resources during a health crisis. Because we are not exclusively spiritual beings like angels, however, an exclusively spiritual approach to illness is often insufficient. We need the help of doctors, counselors, pastors, and other professionals who have skills that can help put us on the road to recovery. God has given these people special gifts to facilitate healing; God offers them to us as gifts when we need them.

As I was preparing this book, a young woman from a fundamentalist denomination asked to see me. She was suffering from major depression and had made several suicidal gestures. Here she was, a born-again Christian who had given her life completely to God, yet prayer, Scripture reading, worship, and constant listening to religious music were not driving the depression from her life. She was devastated. Was God displeased with her? Was her faith weak? Was she doing something wrong?

When I investigated her family history, I found a great deal of depression. I referred her to a community mental-health agency where a staff psychiatrist prescribed an antidepressant and where she gets regular counseling. She is doing well.

When it comes to the treatment of depression, we need all the help we can get. Our spiritual resources can provide significant assistance in combatting depression, especially when they are united with other forms of treatment. Faith heals, but God is not displeased when faith is given a boost by calling upon other allies that facilitate healing. God makes all things work together for good in our lives.

Depression does not mean that we put life on hold. Depression makes us want to run and hide, to stop the world and get off for a while. We cannot and must not! We can't just wait until we are feeling good to do things. When we are depressed, we need to force ourselves to participate in life anyway.

There were numerous days when I was so severely depressed that I found myself praying for the grace to merely survive. Yet, I never missed a day of work or an appointment. I forced myself to function, even when all I wanted to do was go back to bed and sleep for the rest of the day.

There are times when we must go on despite the severe mental pain, because to give in to the pain and withdraw from life is to regress further, giving the illness more power.

None of us can expect to be depression-free all the time. Depression is part of our human condition. We cannot be upbeat and happy all the time. Temporary depression is a normal response to loss, painful experiences, or crises. It is as normal as joy.

Having a bad day at work, or worse yet, losing your job, experiencing the death of a friend or loved one, moving away from those you cherish: all these events and many more can bring feelings of deep sadness and often a temporary state of depression. We *should* be depressed under these circumstances.

With the passage of time, however, we recover. We involve ourselves in daily activities, talk things over with friends or family members, and look to tomorrow. Eventually, the depression lifts.

When the depression persists and begins to impair our functioning, we have gone beyond having the blues to something more serious. It's time to ask for help. Because the transition from normal to abnormal depression can take place so subtly and quietly, it is important to recognize the signs and symptoms of severe depression. (See Warning Signs of Serious Depression, page 94.)

More education about depression and mental illness is needed.
There remain incredible myths and appalling ignorances about depression. For example, few people today would identify depression as an illness. Rather, depression is viewed as some kind of personal weakness that a little will power can banish. Some people think that seeking help is a waste of time and money—that "toughing it out" is all it takes.

Depression is the "common cold" of psychiatric disorders, although it is actually more treatable than the common cold. National statistics indicate that in any given six months, at least ten million Americans experience some form of depressive illness. In varying degrees of intensity, it is a universal experience in all of us, yet only one in five people actually seeks professional help.

Educating people about depression—which certainly is one of the purposes of this book—will make the illness more "respectable," thus making depressed persons more likely to reach out for help. Education about depression can and does save lives.

Depression teaches compassion. *Compassion* literally means "to suffer together." It is not that I lacked compassion for those who suffer. In fact, because of my family history, I had a deep compassion for anyone hurting and especially for the emotionally disturbed.

Since my own experience of depression and pain, however, I have become more compassionate; I am more empathic. When severely depressed persons tell me that they want to die, I know exactly what they are feeling; I've been there.

Suffering breaks down our narcissism, our immature and unhealthy self-love. It is the great equalizer. Once we have suffered, we are bonded to others who suffer.

Because of my own experience, I can commiserate with and support those who are depressed. I can be more helpful to them professionally because I now have a far better sense of what works to facilitate recovery—all flowing out of the crisis I went through myself.

A person suffering from depression needs warm human contact and support. Isolation impedes recovery; we do not heal alone. We need others to help us through the recovery process. In the therapeutic relationship I had with my doctor and psychotherapist, I found much of what I needed to support me along the journey back to wholeness.

For most of my ten-month crisis, I lived with two other priests. I shared none of my struggle with them; in fact, I went to great measures to be sure they didn't see my struggle. Consequently, they were not able to support me. Living in a house with someone is not enough; participating in a loving, caring relationship is imperative to recovery.

Research has shown that if one spouse is depressed and the other is hostile and critical, relapse is inevitable. Weak marriage relationships inhibit recovery; good marriage relationships reduce depression.

Groups like Emotions Anonymous offer a warm, nonjudgmental atmosphere where those hurting are readily accepted. Some parishes have organized similar support groups because they recognize the value of people with the same affliction helping one another.

Warm human contact and consistent caring support are essentials for recovery from depression. Social isolation and withdrawal only serve to "feed" the illness and reduce the effectiveness of treatment.

Hope helps heal depression. Many persons who are severely depressed continue on because they have at least a thin thread of hope. Hope heals hopelessness, the hopelessness that lies at the heart of depression that destroys.

One of the most important functions of both the physician and the therapist who treat depression is to instill in the patient a sense of hope. Hope provides a road out of despair. It tells the suffering person to believe in the reality of better things. Hope believes that recovery from depression is possible.

In my battle with depression, I lost hope—then regained it. When it left me, there seemed to be no reason to go on. When it returned, I sensed that my recovery had begun in earnest. I am living testimony that hope truly does heal.

These basic facts about depression will direct your own recovery or will help you support someone else in his or hers. By God's grace and power, we can come forth from the darkest of tombs into the light and live again.

CONCLUDING COMMENTS

RESOURCES

Concluding Comments

I have written other books on other topics, but this has been the most difficult one to write. Several times, I almost abandoned the project; I'm glad I didn't.

By nature, I am a private person, so the self-disclosure contained in this book has not come easy for me. Baring my soul the way I have and sharing with you the dysfunctions and disorders of my mind have been painful, even with the protection of a pseudonym. So why didn't I quit? Why did I keep going? Why did I complete the project?

This book is essentially linked to the way I see myself. Ever since I was ordained a deacon, I have viewed myself as a healer. If I had not become a clergyman, I probably would have studied medicine.

For years, I asked God for the gift of physical healing because I ministered to so many physically ill people. I was denied that gift. Instead, I was blessed with the gift for inner healing: mind and soul healing. My own experience with major depression has served to enhance and enrich that gift.

This book, then, has grown out of my desire to continue to be an instrument of God's healing power working in and through me. I completed the project because it is my hope that by reading my story, others who suffer from similar emotional disorders—or know those who do—will find hope.

A book such as this can save hurting people considerable time by pointing them in a direction that leads to the help they need. There can be many detours and dead ends on the road to recovery. In these pages, I have tried to provide a road map that will enable the reader to avoid most of them.

For those of you who have similarly come apart and found yourself steeped in the seemingly impenetrable emotional darkness of depression, I offer this prayer: that you may find a lifeline out of the depths of despair into the light of hope and healing.

You can come together again.

Warning Signs of Serious Depression

- General feelings of sadness, emptiness, hopelessness, helplessness, and anxiety
- Sleep disturbances such as insomnia, sleeping too much, or waking up too early
- Decreased appetite with weight loss or increased appetite with weight gain
- Persistent thoughts of death; planning one's suicide; or actual suicidal attempts
- Inappropriate feelings of guilt, shame, and worthlessness; loss of self-esteem
- Loss of interest in pleasurable activities
- Difficulty in concentrating, remembering, and making decisions
- Excessive crying
- Decreased energy; feelings of exhaustion, fatigue, and listlessness
- Chronic aches and pains that do not seem to have a physical cause and do not respond to treatment
- Irritability
- Social withdrawal and isolation

Resources

Often, people who suffer depression don't know where to begin to find help. The following resources offer direction and spedific contacts.

Where to Find Help

- Your pastor or someone on the parish pastoral team: They probably will not be able to treat your depression, but they can refer you to someone who can.
- Your family doctor: If you don't have one, get one.
- Catholic Charities
- Community mental-health agencies
- Psychiatrists, psychologists, clinical social workers

(Check your Yellow Pages under Mental Health Services.)

Where to Get Information About Depression

- Your public library
- Your local mental-health association
- Community mental health centers
- Write to
  National Mental Health Association
  1021 Prince Street
  Alexandria, VA 22314
  800-969-6642

The National Alliance for the Mentally Ill (NAMI)
P.O. Box NAMI-Depression
Arlington, VA 22216

Depression/Awareness, Recognition, Treatment
    (D/ART)
National Institute of Mental Health
5600 Fishers Lane, Room 10-85
Rockville, MD 20857

National Foundation for Depressive Illness
800-248-4344